What Kind of Supervisor Do You Want to Be?

The First Book a Supervisor Should Read

Joseph Swerdzewski

Copyright © 2021 by Joseph Swerdzewski
All rights reserved. This book, or parts thereof, may not be reproduced in any form without written permission from the author/publisher.

Printed in the United States of America
First Edition Printed 2021

ISBN:	978-0-9910121-8-3
Written by:	Joseph Swerdzewski
Edited by:	Jessica Hope Jordan
Cover design by:	Nina Soden
Layout by:	Nina Soden
Published by:	Joseph Swerdzewski

ATTENTION CORPORATIONS, UNIVERSITIES, COLLEGES, AND PROFESSIONAL ORGANIZATIONS: Quantity discounts are available on bulk purchases of this book for educational, or training purposes. Special books or book excerpts can also be created to fit specific needs.

FOR MORE INFORMATION ABOUT
JSA's Books and/or Learning Materials for Organizations
1-256-503-2226
Joseph Swerdzewski
6585 Highway 431 South
Suite E 457
Hampton Cove, AL 35763

Dedication

To all the Supervisors in my family Tom, Brandi, Eric, Nina, Jonathan, Amy, Matt and Barbara.

Table of Contents

Introduction 1

Chapter 1: Personality vs. Communication 5

Chapter 2: The Supervisor as Communicator 10

Chapter 3: The Essential Elements of Communication 18

Chapter 4: Meetings 30

Chapter 5: To Email or Not to Email 35

Chapter 6: Counseling Employees 38

Chapter 7: Discipline 44

Chapter 8: The Supervisor as Investigator 54

Chapter 9: Managing Performance 59

Chapter 10: The Supervisor as Motivator 66

Chapter 11: What Do You Know about Employment Law and Discrimination? 73

Chapter 12: Things Supervisors Should Not Do 83

Chapter 13: A Good Supervisor Has a Philosophy 88

Chapter 14 What Do I Do Now? 98

Introduction

This book assumes that you are a new supervisor, or perhaps you have already been a supervisor for some time. If you are a new supervisor, this book offers you the opportunity to become the kind of supervisor you want to be. If you already are a supervisor, this book will assist you in making significant changes that will greatly improve your supervisory skills, thus making you a better supervisor overall.

The hard work of supervising employees can be both difficult and rewarding. In addition, as is often the case, many new supervisors do not receive much training. Or, as it more frequently happens, they may receive no training at all. All too often new supervisors are just selected, and then just told to go supervise. When this occurs, learning to supervise can then become a kind of sink or swim on-the-job training program. Similarly, those who have been supervising for some time without proper training may have developed poor supervisory practices, or at the least, several less than effective ones. Sometimes, the only training a new supervisor may receive is what they have learned from previous supervisors. This type of passed down training can be either good, bad, or a mix of the two. However, skills-based training, which is discussed in the following chapters, is important for all supervisors, in addition to developing the necessary philosophy and attitudes towards their supervisory duties.

As it happens, a supervisor often emerges as a combination of the type of person the individual may be, the training they have received, and their priorities as a supervisor. What shapes a supervisor further is also the individual's (and to some extent the employer's) philosophy of management. It is a truism that no book or course of training can fully change the kind of person you may be. For example, if you are an introvert, there is no training that can entirely convert you to being an extrovert. You are who you are. However, what can be accomplished is developing an understanding of the ways in which you use the qualities you already possess both to your advantage as a supervisor and for the employees you supervise.

It could be the case that much of the previous supervisory training you may have received has been mostly ignored or was not directly applicable to your needs. This is because the training you should have received would have further educated you on the philosophy and attitudes needed to be a good supervisor, in addition to providing you with specific skills-based training. It is important to note, however, that becoming a good supervisor takes time. To begin with, you must decide that you are willing to allocate the time necessary. Of course, if you already are a supervisor, you likely have many competing responsibilities that may not allow for much extra time. How a supervisor allocates time often depends upon their philosophy as a supervisor. In other words, you get to choose what kind of supervisor you want to be. The priority you place on your role as a supervisor will directly affect the outcomes you obtain. Far too often, however, too many supervisors do not even know what their philosophy of management is, or that they even have a choice.

This information in this book will provide you with several choices for the kind of supervisor you want to be. In doing so, this book is divided into the following four major sections:

1. Communicating with Employees
2. Performance and Conduct of Employees
3. Supervising the Work of Employees
4. Your Philosophy of Supervision

Each of these major sections contain several subdivisions. As you explore the qualities and skills necessary to being a good supervisor, you will find that you will have to make choices about what kind of supervisor you want to be.

The most fundamental question for a supervisor to ask is what are you supposed to be doing in your role as a supervisor? Of course, you know that you are supposed to be supervising employees, and you also know you are supposed to get the job done. However, is it possible that you need to know something more?

Here is a list of tasks supervisors commonly perform:

- Supervise employees
- Assign work to employees
- Communicate with employees
- Conduct meetings with employees
- Counsel employees
- Investigate employee misconduct
- Discipline employees
- Develop employee performance standards
- Evaluate employees
- Motivate employees
- Improve employee job performance
- Assist employees in career development

- Know the laws and rules that apply to employees

How much do you already know about how to accomplish these tasks? How important is it for you to be considered a good supervisor? Because becoming a good supervisor will increase the respect of the employees you supervise as well as greatly assist you in accomplishing the job, answering these fundamental questions first is important.

Traditionally, the essential role of a supervisor has been to accomplish the mission, while meeting the strategic goals of the company. This entails, on an almost a daily basis, making many decisions about the work their employees do. And the kinds of decisions a supervisor makes stems from their personal decisions about what kind of supervisor they want to be.

As you begin this book you should know that, while the ways in which you act as a supervisor are not preordained, much of your approach to supervising employees, as well as your success as a supervisor, is based on the choices you make. After reading this book, you will be able to make the right choices.

Chapter 1
Personality vs. Communication

Let us begin by considering how important your personality is in determining whether you will be a good supervisor. Naturally, everyone has a personality: some people are quiet, some are loud, some are thoughtful, and some are thoughtless, with many variations in between. You may wonder whether to be an effective supervisor if you have to be outgoing and extroverted, or should you be pensive and quiet-spoken? Should your personality be a key determinant for your selection as a supervisor? Can you, or should you, do anything about the way you already are to improve your chances of becoming a good supervisor?

You may already be familiar with how employment agencies and companies often have potential employees take personality tests. These tests are also often given once you are employed. One of the most frequently used tests is the Myers-Briggs Personality Test. The Myers-Briggs test can provide a better understanding of why people act and speak in certain ways, which, in turn, can allow you both to relate more to others and to communicate more effectively with them. It also provides insights into how you may be perceived by others.

The Myers-Briggs Type Indicator (MBTI) is an especially helpful tool for understanding and categorizing personality archetypes. The test is based on the following main characteristics: Introversion/Extroversion, Intuition/Sensing, Feeling/Thinking, and Judging/Perceiving. Individuals are then categorized into a type based on which of the four traits they demonstrate. After taking the Myers-Briggs test, you can find out which of sixteen different personality types fits you.

For example, if you are an INTP this means you are Introverted, Intuitive, Thinking, and Perceiving. Individuals who are introverted draw energy from time spent by themselves. They are usually less talkative and more emotionally reserved. **Introverts** generally prefer to be alone, so others should focus on being respectful of an introvert's time, while also communicating clearly. Those who identify more with the **Intuition** characteristic love to explore new ideas. They enjoy seeing how everything connects and demonstrate strong instincts. Intuitive types generally prefer thinking about the bigger picture, so it is best to avoid focusing too heavily on the details. Those who are **Thinking** types prefer thinking logically and considering the facts when making decisions. Thinking types prefer direct and honest communication, so it is best to avoid being overly emotional. Individuals who identify with the **Perceiving** characteristic prefer to be flexible and spontaneous. They dislike rigid rules and processes, preferring instead to go with the flow. Perceiving types do not like to feel controlled, so it is best to focus on being encouraging and upbeat.

The application of Myers-Briggs types can help you better to understand why individuals act and speak in certain ways, and, in turn, this will allow you both to relate more to others and to communicate more effectively with them. There are fifteen other personality types, one of which may fit you. Once you figure out your personality type, the theory is that this should help you to be able to communicate more effectively with people who have one of the other personality types. The Myers Briggs test is available free online: www.my-personality-test.com/free/myersbriggs

While the Myers Briggs Test helps you to understand both your own and other's personalities, it neither makes you a better communicator nor does it suggest that you can change your personality. While some individuals are known as a "people person," or as someone who enjoys or who is particularly good at interacting with others, not everyone is a people person. Fortunately, being a good supervisor does not mean you must become a people person. Instead, you must take the personality you have and use it to your best advantage. However, you may find that you still do have to adapt some of the ways you interact with others to be successful. If you are an introvert, however, it does not mean that you need a personality transplant to be something you are not. If you are an extrovert, it does not mean that you have to change; instead, you may only have to learn when and how to act differently when necessary.

For instance, I remember the first time I took the Myers Briggs Personality Test. It was during a seminar at a training facility in Charlottesville, Virginia. Before they handed out the results to everyone in the class, they called me into a meeting with the school's expert on Myers Briggs. He told me that I was off the charts for being an introvert. He had seen very few people, if any, score so strongly as an introvert. He asked me what I did. I told him I was a trial lawyer, supervisor, and did a lot of training. He asked me how I handled what he called my "extreme introversion," in doing my job. I told him that each day I knew I had to interact with people in whatever role I was performing, and that to do my job I had to be a different person than I otherwise may have liked to be. At the end of performing the role, however, I knew I could go back to being the way I was.

If you just do not like interacting with people, being a supervisor may not be for you. It is true that you can learn how to deal effectively with people regardless of your personality type. However, if you are just not interested in interacting with others, supervising may not be something that will work well for you or the employees you would be supervising. A person who does not want to talk to other people will necessarily have a hard time being a good communicator. Nevertheless, one thing to understand is that your personality type does not make you either a good or bad communicator. For instance, an introvert can be a great communicator. Introverts who find direct interaction difficult can become effective communicators by simply pretending to be extroverted for short periods of time, such as when engaging with an employee. In contrast, an extrovert can be a terrible communicator because they may fail to spend the time necessary to make certain their communications are both clearly understood and effective. Everyone can learn to be a good communicator—that is, if they want to be one. While it is difficult, if not impossible, to change your personality, anyone can improve their communication skills to be the kind of supervisor they want to be.

If you want to be a good supervisor, then, you must first decide whether you want to interact with employees. If you realize that interacting with employees is not something you want to do, then perhaps think about other career choices instead of being a supervisor. However, if you still want to be a supervisor, it is important to realize that you are not being asked to be a people person or to become an extrovert overnight. The real question is are you willing to learn how to be effective when interacting with employees? If the answer is, yes, I want to be effective in my interactions with employees, then you can learn how to communicate effectively regardless of what Myers Briggs has designated as your personality.

These are your choices:

1. **You cannot easily change your personality, but you can choose to be effective when interacting with employees.**

2. **You do not have to be a "people person," but you can choose to be an effective communicator.**

Chapter 2
The Supervisor as Communicator

If, as a supervisor, you have chosen to be effective when interacting with your employees, communication is the most important method for success. As previously mentioned, being a people person is not the sole answer to being a good supervisor; however, being a good communicator is. Of course, because you already know how to talk and how to write, you already are a communicator. However, how often you choose to communicate with your employees, as well as how effective the method of communication you choose may be, are important decisions you must make.

The National Communication Association assessed how effective communication is in the workplace, with the following results:

- Sixty-nine percent of employees are comfortable talking with co-workers.
- Fifty-seven percent of employees are comfortable talking with their boss.
- Forty-two percent of employees think their bosses are effective communicators.

Based on these percentage values, it is easy to see that these are not great marks for supervisory communication. How many of those 43% of employees who do not feel comfortable talking with their boss work may for you? How well do the employees you supervise rate you as a communicator? Is there an area of communication with your employees that you may need to work on?

Assess What Kind of Communicator You Are

Performing a simple assessment of how your employees view communication at your workplace can be helpful for identifying ways to improve workplace communication. Such an assessment of the communication in a workplace relationship allows participants to gain an understanding of everyone's perspectives and experiences. It can also be a useful tool to improve communication or to deal with workplace conflict. A communication assessment's main purpose is to give everyone who is in a communication relationship an opportunity to express their beliefs about the effectiveness of their communication.

I have used the assessment provided in this chapter on many occasions where there have been conflicts in the workplace, or as a way to build more powerful communication in long established relationships. This assessment is intended to be a simple way to gain an understanding of the current beliefs of the participants about how effective communication is in the workplace. It does not pretend to be a scientific survey; instead, it is a quick way to find out how the participants perceive the effectiveness of communication. Whether there are conflicts or not, this assessment can be helpful in giving all participants an insight into how communication is looked at by all participants. It also is a first step for beginning the process of developing ways to create more effective communication.

Two Phases of the Assessment

There are two phases to this assessment: The first phase is the rating each participant provides for the effectiveness of communication. The second phase is discussing the results of the assessment, including why various participants rated communication the way they did. How these two phases are conducted is important. In a highly conflicted workplace, employees are frequently reluctant to confront their manager with how they feel about how things are going in the workplace for fear of reprisal.

One approach for obtaining the ratings is to have each participant place their rating on a piece of paper without disclosing their name. These ratings are then given to the facilitator, who places them on the chart used to tabulate the ratings. This allows anonymity for the rater. Another approach is to have each participate verbally relate their rating. The vast majority of participants in a communication assessment will willingly give their ratings verbally as well as fully participate in a discussion of the results. However, in some rare circumstances, the first approach may be preferable to the participants.

Ground Rules for the Assessment

Establishing ground rules for the assessment can help participants to feel more secure when sharing their opinions. Although the assessment is intended to deal with improving communication, it is frequently the case that other issues are discussed as part of the assessment process. Some of these issues may be difficult for employees to discuss. Ground rules should therefore be established and agreed upon before beginning the assessment. The supervisor and/or facilitator should explain the following ground rules:

- The purpose of the assessment is to improve the communication in the workplace.
- In determining your rating, the participants should use their overall viewpoint on the effectiveness of workplace communication.
- All participants should feel free to speak candidly and honestly at all times.
- The normal rules of courtesy and civility will be maintained. This includes, but is not limited to, refraining from interrupting someone who is speaking and being respectful of one other.
- Ask if there are any other ground rules that need to be added.

The Assessment

The assessment is a simple five-step process that can be completed in 30–45 minutes, depending on the number of participants in the assessment:

1. Explain the ground rules to help participants feel comfortable as well as to provide structure for the discussion. At the same time, in view of all the participants, display the assessment chart (below) on a flipchart or white board.

Communication Assessment

1	5	10
Extremely Poor		Extremely Good

2. Ask participants to reflect on the systems and processes currently used to communicate with one another. Participants should silently rate how effective they believe communication is in the workplace on a 1–10 scale, with 1 indicating extremely poor communication, and 10 indicating extremely good communication. Participants are asked either to write their rating on a piece of paper and give it to the supervisor/facilitator or one-by-one announce their rating. As the ratings are given by the participants, the supervisor/facilitator will place a mark on the chart where the rating fits. As an example, if the rating is a 3, then the supervisor/facilitator will place a mark on the chart approximately where a rating of 3 would fit. Participants should not explain the reasoning behind their rating at this time.

3. When all participants have placed a mark on the assessment chart, ask each one to explain their rating. This can lead to considerable discussion about workplace issues not strictly related to communication. The supervisor/facilitator should be prepared to facilitate this discussion.

4. After each participant has answered, ask for suggestions for actions that can be taken to improve communication.

5. Formulate a plan of action to implement the suggested actions that can be taken. (After this step, participants should also review Chapter 3 to consider additional ideas and actions to improve communication.)

As many know, today's workplace is not always an office where everyone works together. Today, it is just as likely for an employee to work in their home many miles from their duty station. In this work arrangement, an employee's interaction with their boss and fellow employees is usually by telephone or email. Telework or remote work, which is synonymous with the term "telecommute," is when employees perform their job functions from locations outside of a traditional office environment. Increasingly more work is being done by employees who telework. This makes communication even more important.

Communication is a Two-Way Street

Communication in a supervisor-employee relationship should always be a two-way street, and both the supervisor and the employee have responsibilities to communicate. The employee must understand that they have as much responsibility to communicate with the supervisor as the supervisor has to communicate to the employee. In return, the supervisor must encourage employees to communicate as well as to provide the means and processes for their communication.

Within a normal supervisor-employee relationship, the supervisor must be prepared to effectively communicate to the employee the following:

- Directions about what work is to be performed and how
- Expectations about how much and when work is to be completed, and to what standards
- Corrections for the employee's performance and conduct

Similarly, within a normal supervisor-employee relationship, an employee must be able to communicate the following:

- When directions are not understood, or certain tasks cannot be performed
- When expectations are not understood, or cannot be met
- When personal or other problems affect performance or conduct

It is unfortunate, however, that in some supervisor-employee relationships, the only time communication takes place is when it is absolutely required as part of a performance or disciplinary process. For this reason, each employee and supervisor should ask themselves how much of their communication actually takes place outside of these formal processes. While these processes usually specify the minimal communication, as well as the requirements expected of supervisors and employees, it is also often the case that these minimal requirements are not even being met.

While much time is often spent focusing on supervisor-employee communication, all too frequently, an important relationship is overlooked: communication between supervisors and managers. Consider, for a moment, how well do supervisors and managers communicate with each other? Much of what is said about communication between supervisors and employees can also apply to the supervisor-manager relationship. It is just as important that the supervisor-manager relationship have effective communication and trust as it is for the supervisor and employee relationship. As it happens, in many organizations, improving this key relationship is too often overlooked.

These are your choices:

1. You can choose to be a good communicator.

2. You can choose to find out what your employees think of you as a communicator.

3. You can choose to go beyond the minimal communication expected in the workplace

Chapter 3
The Essential Elements of Communication

During my career, my extensive work with both employee-supervisor and union-management relationships has helped me to uncover four foundational elements that make communication successful in the workplace: attitude, skill, process, and quality. By working on each of these elements, you can become an effective communicator. Communication is hard work. It takes determination and skill to be considered a good communicator. To be willing to put the time in that is needed to be a communicator will be one of the major decisions you will have to make if you want to be a good supervisor. How much time and effort are you willing to put in to improve your communication capabilities? Many supervisors are not aware that the employees they supervise are continually assessing their skills of communication as a supervisor. When reading this chapter, consider further how supervisors and employees can benefit from improved communication skills.

What follows explains the **Four Essential Elements of Communication—Attitude, Skill, Process, and Quality:**

1. Attitude: Willingness to communicate

A willingness to communicate is one of the most essential elements of effective communication. Only those who are willing to communicate are able to work to improve their skills, processes, and quality of communication.

There are a variety of reasons for a lack of communication with employees by supervisors. The most common reason cited by supervisors is that they are just too busy. It takes time to communicate, and supervisors often have their own work to do. It is not that supervisors do not want to communicate, but there is often just not enough time both to accomplish their work and spend time communicating with employees. Unfortunately, for many supervisors and managers, they often also have a full load of the work as do the employees, and supervising is just an add-on which brings them a higher salary. However, not taking the time to communicate is a version of not being willing to communicate. If communication is not a priority, it is no different than not being willing to engage with employees.

Employees and supervisors frequently erect barriers that intentionally or unintentionally impede paths to improved work relationships. Many may also allow past experiences to impact future communication. These barriers and past experiences, however, have the effect of excess baggage, and discarding it is rarely easy. Baggage is defined as those past experiences that have had such a negative effect on many people that they continue to carry the baggage around with them, and they often have difficulty ever unloading it. These past experiences frequently govern how an individual makes decisions about both the present and future. Baggage can also make people fearful or reluctant to communicate with someone whom they have perceived to have treated them unfairly in the past, or who, as a result of the previous interaction, is no longer trusted.

Some individuals may have been carrying around such baggage from previous work relationships for a long time. For example, at a relationship building program I was facilitating, a manager was finally able to discuss what he considered to be unfair treatment by another manager that had taken place over ten years before. This past interaction had constantly guided his dealings with his current fellow manager. Usually, many who are in a work relationship are aware of an interaction that created a conflict. However, a supervisor may not even be aware of the nature of the baggage employees have been carrying around with them or the extent that trust has been eroded.

With all the responsibilities faced by a supervisor, it is important to ask how often supervisors actually speak with employees each week. It is equally important to ask how employees could answer a similar question. It is important to note here that, in most cases, employees neither expect nor want a supervisor to communicate with them in the ways and with the frequency they communicate with friends. The supervisor-employee relationship is not a friendship and should not be treated as such. Supervisors should not treat employees as friends. While a friendship may in some ways help communication, it could just as easily undermine a supervisor's ability to maintain a business relationship in the workplace. Friendships between supervisors and employees also frequently lead to beliefs by other employees who are not considered to be a "friend" of the supervisor that favoritism exists with the supervisor's friends. Therefore, instead of friendships, communication between a supervisor and employees should be conducted as a business relationship between respected colleagues.

To Do List:

Keep track of how many times over the next two weeks you communicate with each of the employees you supervise. If you are a spreadsheet person, you will especially like this activity. Create a chart with the employee's name, and then place a mark aside their name each time you talk to the employee or send the employee a text message or an email or respond to their text or email. This will give you a good idea of how much interaction takes place and will reveal important patterns, such as: Are there some employees you talk with more than others? If so, then the question you have to ask is why this occurs. Do you talk with them more often because it is work-related or because they are easier to talk with? What about the employees you talk with less often? Is it because they do not need as much help or because you just do not like them? Did this chart further reveal that you used email considerably more than verbal communication or vice versa?

Based on the information this chart provides, what are you willing to do to increase communication where it is needed as well as change the method of communication where it is needed? Once you have determined this, you will additionally have to find the right balance between verbal and electronic communication.

2. Skill: Ability to communicate

Communication is the exchange and flow of ideas from one person to another. Effective communication occurs only when a recipient correctly understands information in ways that a sender has intended. While these fundamental aspects of communication may be easy to understand, exercising the necessary skills and becoming good at communicating can still be challenging. Good communication skills are necessary not only for managers, but also for employees. Many of the problems faced by employees in the workplace result from their own inadequate communication skills. While an organization's management may invest training dollars in improving supervisors' communication skills, employees, however, rarely receive the same training opportunities.

There are **Four Essential Skills for Effective Communication—Listening, Verbal, Non-Verbal, and Written**:

a. Listening skills – This is the most often used communication skill, but usually the least developed. Being a good listener is an important skill for all supervisors. When you listen, do you give the speaker the impression that you are both listening to and understanding what they are saying? We live in a country that values multitaskers, or being able to do more than one thing at the same time. Effective listening, however, does not lend itself well to multitasking. A speaker can clearly get the impression that your mind is somewhere else, which, to be honest, it probably is. Listening, however, means truly concentrating on what someone is saying. Listening does not mean that you have to agree with what is being said; however, you do have to acknowledge that you understand what the speaker is trying to convey. If you want to dazzle your employees, dazzle them with your ability to listen to them.

b. Verbal skills – Most everyone knows how to talk. However, not everyone is comfortable giving a speech. Most supervisors will not be called upon to speak in front of hundreds of employees, but you will have to speak to your own employees. This communication may be conducted informally in a person-to-person conversation or more formally in a meeting with all the employees you supervise. The most important thing to do when speaking is be prepared by considering beforehand what you are going to say. If you do not spend the time figuring out what you want your employees to take away from your talk, you will be a poor communicator. Here, it is especially important to note that offhand unplanned remarks can often lead to miscommunication, and sometimes even much worse outcomes.

c. Nonverbal skills – These are some of the most powerful ways of getting your message across to your employees. Nonverbal communication, also known as body language, is an important mode of communication. All the employees in an office usually know when the boss is having a bad day. The boss does not even have to say anything. It is apparent in the way they act. For this reason, it is important to be mindful of the message you are conveying to your employees, even when you are not talking to them. According to Albert Mehrabian in his book, **Silent Messages** (1971), during a conversation it is interesting to note that words alone are only 7% effective, a speaker's tone of voice is 38% effective, while their nonverbal cues are 55% effective. Nonverbal cues include elements of body language, such as crossing one's arms or sitting, as well as both the speaker and the listener's emotional indicators, for example, whispering, shouting, or speaking enthusiastically.

The way one listens, looks, moves, and reacts further tells the other person whether or not the speaker cares, whether or not they are being truthful, and how well they are listening. When nonverbal signals match up with words, body language and tone of voice can increase rapport. When nonverbal signals and words are incompatible, tension, mistrust, and confusion can occur. When approaching employees, posture, facial expressions, and other physical cues must match the words being spoken. These are things you can control. Therefore, be certain to prepare not only what will be said, but also how it will be said through your tone of voice and body language, and especially your facial expressions.

d. Written skills – These are often the most frequently taught communication skills. More time is often spent teaching people how to write than on any other communication skill. With writing it is not a question of only knowing how to write, but also how to be an effective writer. Although many of us were taught how to write through formal education, writing can remain one of the most difficult areas for successful communication. The simplest way to improve your writing, however, is to take the time to plan out what you want to convey. This means that rushing to write an email can quickly turn into disaster once you realize that the one you sent was not really the one you wanted received.

To Do List:

Practice the following effective listening techniques with your spouse or friends:

- **Paraphrase:** Restate in your own words what the other person has said to show you are listening.
- **Clarify:** Ask questions in order to give strong feedback that shows you are trying hard to understand the other person's statements.
- **Check perceptions**: Verify with the speaker not only the content of the conversation, but also whether or not you correctly perceived and understood what was said.
- **Summarize:** Briefly sum up the conversation to show that you have been listening, while allowing the speaker to correct your interpretation.

3. **Process: Way(s) of exchanging information –**
Communication processes in the workplace can be formal or informal. Formal processes usually include unwritten, while nevertheless understood, ground rules or other norms that clarify how, when, where, why, and among whom certain communications take place. For example, a staff meeting can be a formal communication process because it usually occurs at a scheduled time, with a

predetermined agenda set by the supervisor, and takes place in a set location. Everyone attending a staff meeting usually understands their role in the communication. In contrast, informal communication is unstructured and can take place at any time and in any place. For example, chatting between supervisors in an office hallway, or stopping by an employee's desk with questions, are two such informal processes.

To establish effective communication in the workplace, both supervisors *and* employees must use formal and informal processes, and supervisors must further decide which to use when communicating with employees. Should the supervisor communicate face-to-face, by phone, through email, text, or via videoconference, among other choices? How should a supervisor address rumors, which are only one type of informal communication? If you find yourself only communicating using one process, such as email, you may be losing opportunities to develop a better relationship with your employees by using face-to-face and other verbal communication processes.

4. Quality: Essential character and value of exchanged information

How many meetings have you attended that were an absolute waste of time? How many reports have you read that were impossible to understand? How many mornings do you arrive at work and already have one hundred emails in your inbox? Most of us are bombarded with information on a daily basis. What we should be asking ourselves, however, is "How much of this is *high-quality information?*"

One may have a workplace that meets three of the Essential Elements for Effective Communication: 1) **Attitude**, or willingness to communicate; 2) **Skill**, or ability to communicate; and 3) **Process**, or way(s) of exchanging information. However, the workplace may still fall short when it comes to the fourth element: **Quality**, or the essential character and value of information exchanged. Quality can be difficult to define. Many of us know quality work when we see it; however, describing our measures for assessing quality can be difficult. Having guided many managers on implementing performance management systems, I have found that most supervisors are not quite able to put into words their expectations for the quality of an employee's work. As a result, employees often do not understand what is expected of them.

To avoid a similar situation, it helps to consider the following **Three Measures of Quality for Good Communication—Understood by Recipient, Concise, and Precise Vocabulary:**

1. Understood by Recipient

Quality communication is communicating in ways that another person understands. The most important measure of quality communication is whether your message can be understood by its recipients. If one has doubts on this point, ask the other person to paraphrase the conversation in their own words.

2. Concise

Is a writer using ten words when just one will do? Quantity is not a measure of quality communication. Are words constantly being repeated? Sometimes, repetition can help to emphasize a message; however, unnecessary repetition can have the opposite effect. Ensure conciseness by practicing a conversation in advance. Do practice sessions reveal repetition, vagueness, or disorganized thinking? Unless one is being paid by the word—and most supervisors and employees are not—use as few words as possible, while aiming for accuracy. More is not necessarily better when it comes to communication. Bombarding an employee with lengthy emails may have the opposite effect of supplying more information than is needed, while resulting in an employee failing to read the voluminous emails.

3. Precise Vocabulary

Make certain the vocabulary is appropriate for the audience. Are acronyms and highly-specialized language being used? If the audience is not familiar with acronyms or industry jargon, then be certain to explain what they mean.

When assessing your communication skills, you may realize that you do not possess equal abilities in all four areas. You may be a better writer, while others are better speakers. Not all supervisors have the same aptitudes. Although supervisors and employees are not expected to be equally skilled, all workplace participants must have enough reading and writing skills to communicate effectively. You must work on those skills that need to be improved.

To sum it all up—communication is hard work. It requires a dedicated effort on a continuous basis. However, you can become a good communicator if you choose to be.

These are your choices:

1. **You can choose to make communication with your employees a priority.**

2. **You can choose to take the time necessary to be a good communicator.**

3. **You can choose to improve your communication skills.**

Chapter 4
Meetings

While every supervisor conducts meetings of different types, the most common type is a **staff meeting**. Frequently, poorly run staff meetings draw significant criticism from employees. Almost all employees have at one time or another been to a staff meeting that was a complete waste of time. You do not want your staff meetings to be in that category.

Group meetings, including staff meetings, help to establish a broader awareness of organizational activities by sharing information about an organization's big picture. Group meetings are communication processes during which many employees receive information simultaneously, thus allowing employees the ability to act on news at the same time. Every organization should include group meetings as part of an overall communication strategy for disseminating information to employees. Group meetings should be held frequently to allow employees to stay abreast of what is happening in the organization and their work unit. If you do not have the time to plan the meeting, do you have time to waste of each of your employees' time when the meeting does not accomplish its purpose? The plan does not have to be an extensive agenda; it can be as simple as using notes to guide you through the meeting.

What Makes a Good Staff Meeting?

Staff meetings are a common formal communication process used in most workplaces. These are usually scheduled for the same time and location each week. Most often, a supervisor runs the meeting. Some staff meetings will have a pre-ordained length. All of these factors make staff meetings a formal communication process. The real question is of what value are these meetings to the employees? Quite often, staff meetings are dreaded by employees. A staff meeting for the sake of a staff meeting is a waste of time. Common complaints from employees about staff meetings are "the meeting told me nothing of value, it went on way too long, there was no real discussion, just the supervisor going on and on, and if there is nothing to tell us, then why are we here?"

Let's look at some of the things that make a good staff meeting:

Purpose

Does the meeting have a clearly understood purpose and objectives? For example: Is the meeting solely to disseminate information? Or is it to discuss a workplace problem? Is it an instructional meeting to explain a new work process? It is best if the purpose and objectives of the meeting are clearly understood ahead of time by the employees because this gives them an opportunity to prepare, if necessary, but also to consider what is going to be discussed.

Preparation for the meeting.

The more preparation by the supervisor, then the better the meeting will go. If the supervisor is not prepared for the meeting, the meeting will not meet its purpose and objectives. A simple process such as writing notes about what is to be discussed will help to give some structure to the meeting. Such notes can be the basis for a meeting agenda. If there is no time to prepare, then it may be better to reschedule the meeting and set it for a time when the supervisor will be ready.

Length of the Meeting

A staff meeting should have a normally scheduled period of time, so that employees can set aside that time from their other work activities. However, it is not always necessary to use this scheduled time. If there is not enough information to take up the time, then the meeting should end. Rather than just fill up the time allotted, a bigger mistake is to have overly long staff meetings. If the meeting is going to take longer than the normally scheduled time, a special time should be set up with notice to the employees.

Meeting Rules

Having rules for the conduct of the meeting will improve its effectiveness. Simple rules, such as the meeting starting and ending on time, will help employees know that they can plan their day. Whether issues that are not on the agenda can also be brought up will help employees to understand whether the meeting is strictly for the purposes of the agenda or may be open to other issues. Rules that encourage or discourage employee participation will further help them to understand what they should be prepared for at the meeting. If employees have a responsibility to report work progress or work problems, this should also be part of the rules for the meeting. How long such reports should take will also be helpful to employees. A supervisor should always think in terms of what will help the meetings be more successful, including asking employees how to improve the meetings.

One-on-one meetings are just between a supervisor and an employee. It is important to establish ground rules for when employees should seek help from a supervisor, rather than when employees will be expected to solve problems on their own. Ground rules should frequently be repeated, so that employees understand that appropriate communication with supervisors is an important aspect of their jobs. Some areas to establish ground rules for employees can include:

- The best way(s) for employees to make it known that they would like to talk to you
- The best times and places for supervisor-employee discussions
- When email should or should not be used to convey information
- Which issues should be prioritized for communication

You may ask why spend time establishing ground rules? The answer is simple: Because you do not want to be among the supervisors who 42% of employees think are poor communicators.

These are your choices:

1. You can choose to have good staff meetings that are planned in advance and are valuable for both you and your employees.

2. You can choose to have ground rules that make it clear to employees when and how to communicate with you.

Chapter 5
To Email or Not to Email

Today, a large amount of written communication between supervisors and employees takes place using email or other electronic means, such as instant messaging or texting. Tremendous amounts of information can be exchanged by email. Electronic communications allow people to remain in constant contact without ever being in the same room. The widespread use of email in the workplace has led to many organizations adopting virtual offices, allowing employees to work from their homes. For many organizations, the only equipment necessary for conducting work remotely is a computer with Internet access and some type of telephone capability.

Previously, employees were not subjected to the communication alternatives used by supervisors today. Therefore, in the modern workplace, supervisors should carefully consider when to use email for initiating discussions. Dashing off an email to an employee is, of course, much faster than making a telephone call, or walking across an office floor. Email further allows supervisors to contact employees without needing to track them down. Today, many tend to be far less concerned about grammar and punctuation in emails than in formal documents. Many of us believe that emails require far less thought; however, this misbelief can lead to disaster. Emails can cause significant communication problems. In my career as a facilitator and mediator, I have encountered many disputes that were caused by emails.

Recent technological advancements have allowed for a marked increase in telework. Some employees may be in the office only certain days a week, while virtual employees (telecommuters) may be located many states away from their direct supervisors. These new work arrangements pose even greater challenges for effective supervisor-employee communication. An out of sight, out of mind attitude can pose a problem for both supervisors and employees who telework. As will be discussed later, alternative worksite arrangements require just as much communication, if not more, in some circumstances, as typical workplace situations do. While it is easier to email or text an employee who is working from home, verbal communication should be the main mode for how communication is conducted with remote employees.

Applying the following **three basic rules for email use** will help to avoid disputes caused by poor email communication:

> **Rule 1**: Never write anything in an email that you would not say face-to-face. Remember that when sending an email, one will not be able to gauge the recipient's reaction to see what impact the email has had. In addition, there will not necessarily be an opportunity to clarify what was written. Finally, an email is available for a recipient to read over and over again, and potentially to become angrier and angrier. It also can easily be shared with others.
>
> **Rule 2**: If angry, annoyed, or otherwise upset, wait at least an hour before hitting "send." After that time, if it is still necessary to send the email, then go ahead.

Rule 3: When giving an employee bad news, make every effort to deliver it in person. Most believe that breaking off a relationship through email is an unfair approach, although some may find it efficient and less messy. A supervisor can also fire employees through electronic communication but should always question if employees deserve to hear such bad news in this manner. The answer to that question depends on what type of supervisor you want to be.

Email should not be used as a tool for avoiding face-to-face discussion with employees. Resorting to email may seem easy but can actually create additional problems when a supervisor uses it to avoid speaking to an employee. Employees can handle bad news much better than you believe. How the message is presented can change their response. However, email will not allow you to receive instant feedback, and it will not provide an opportunity to explain or soften the words. When applying the above rules, always ask first if email is the best communication method for delivering the intended message.

These are your choices:

1. You can choose to adopt some basic rules about emails sent to your employees.

2. You can choose to use communication processes other than email to deliver difficult news to an employee.

Chapter 6
Counseling Employees

In my experience, supervisors do not correct employee behavior too often, but rather too infrequently, as well as too late. Some supervisors find it easy to show appreciation but more difficult to tackle performance issues. Others find it easy to correct bad behavior but difficult to praise and reward good behavior. By showing appreciation without ever communicating corrections, a supervisor with unexpressed concerns can lead an employee to believe that everything is fine. Employees often say that they believed they were performing at an adequate level, until suddenly receiving a poor performance rating.

When teaching supervisory training classes, I advise supervisors to counsel early and often when it comes to conduct and performance issues. Many supervisors dread counseling their employees. Counseling has a negative connotation when considered a precursor to disciplinary actions. However, counseling that is done well and taken seriously by the employee will actually negate the need for further action. If supervisors want to become effective counselors, they must be prepared for the task. Counseling, however, should not occur in the form of an impromptu discussion. To be effective, an employee counseling session needs to be prepared for.

The following six steps will help to enhance counseling sessions with individual employees:

1. Identify the problem.

What problems require correction? Is the employee frequently tardy? Is the employee missing deadlines on a regular basis? Determine what problem or problems need to be discussed before initiating the meeting. The root causes of the problem should be a central topic. The purpose of the counseling is to try to find out why the problem is occurring and what can be done to cure the problem.

2. Plan, coordinate, and organize the session.

Location is important. Ideally, aim for a confidential discussion that will not be overhead by others. Counseling meetings are not intended to embarrass employees. If the objective is to enforce a conduct rule, then the discussion should take place in the supervisor's office, with the supervisor sitting at his or her desk. If the meeting is designed as a collaborative problem-solving exercise, then the discussion should be held in a neutral location, such as a conference room where the supervisor and employee can sit side-by-side, if they prefer.

As the supervisor, develop a mental plan for the meeting and know ahead of time what is to be accomplished. Do not be tempted to wing it and see how things go. An agenda will help keep the meeting on track, so that the goals are accomplished without running the risk of the employee or you monopolizing the meeting.

3. Be sincere and compassionate, but remain firm and in control.

Yelling at an employee may make you feel better for a moment but will rarely lead to an employee altering his or her behavior in the future. Instead, raising one's voice often creates even higher barriers. If a supervisor is angry with an employee, or if the employee is angry with a supervisor, it is not the right time to conduct a counseling session. It is not unusual for an employee to replicate a supervisor's demeanor during a meeting. Anger will usually only create more anger and/or resentment.

The supervisor must take responsibility for setting the meeting's tone. Sincerity, compassion, and kindness are appropriate when dealing with employee conduct issues. The purpose of counseling is to motivate behavioral changes, and not to create enemies. Try to create an atmosphere in which the employee wants to contribute to the discussion, but remember to remain in control of the session. As mentioned, there should always be ground rules for a counseling session. One of the most important rules is that counseling should always be conducted in a civil manner.

4. Analyze the forces influencing the behavior.

During the session, determine what the employee believes to be the cause of the counterproductive behavior. Try to understand what will be required to change the behavior. Is the employee late for work because they cannot get out of bed on time? Or are they late because of heavy traffic on the way to their child's daycare center? A counseling session is an opportunity both for the supervisor to explain concerns *and* for the employee to explain their side of the story. And employees should feel that their supervisor is listening when the employee explains their situation.

5. Decide whether to use directive or non-directive counseling.

Try to decide when to use directive or non-directive counseling techniques. Directive counseling involves telling the employee what is expected of them. Non-directive counseling is used when a supervisor enlists an employee in suggesting ways to improve. An example of directive counseling would be telling an employee who is consistently tardy that work starts at 9:00 a.m., and that arriving after that time will lead to disciplinary action. Non-directive counseling would be asking the employee why they are always late for work. In this approach, the supervisor should be prepared to define appropriate behaviors, while still engaging the employee in brainstorming ways to improve.

6. Use the facts to decide and explain what actions are required.

No counseling session should end without the supervisor and the employee firmly understanding what decision has been made. The meeting should conclude with the supervisor summarizing any guidance and direction concerning the employee's future conduct or performance. The supervisor must clearly define what is expected and what will happen if these expectations are not met. The employee should then be allowed to ask questions in order to clarify the supervisor's meaning.

Case Study and Exercise: Late Again

Amy has arrived late to five client meetings within the past month. Her clients think highly of her and have not yet complained to Jonathan, Amy's direct supervisor. However, Jonathan recently heard about Amy's behavior from other employees. He has counseled her twice in the past about her tardiness and unscheduled absences. At one of those meetings, Amy became extremely upset and accused Jonathan of unfair treatment. She reminded Jonathan that she had received exceptional customer reviews from her clients.

Jonathan remains concerned about Amy's behavior and wants to address this continuing problem as soon as possible. For this reason, he has asked Amy to join him for a meeting. Jonathan prides himself on providing excellent customer service; however, Amy's attitude reflects poorly on the company. On the morning of their meeting, Amy arrives late to the office for her session with Jonathan.

Using the six steps outlined above, plan for this counseling meeting as if you were in Jonathan's role by asking the following questions:

1. What problem is Jonathan trying to correct? Is it Amy's tardiness to client meetings, her disregard for prior counseling, or her new infraction of arriving late to this

session? How should Jonathan handle the fact that Amy has arrived late to the counseling session?

2. Where should Jonathan hold the meeting in order to ensure that Amy understands the seriousness of the issue?

3. Should Jonathan take a directive counseling approach and make it clear to Amy what the rules are regarding repeat tardiness? Is the goal of the meeting be firm about Amy not being tardy? Or is the meeting an opportunity to work together and find a solution to her tardiness? Depending on the approach you choose, decide what questions one would ask Amy and what directions she should be given.

4. How should Jonathan begin the discussion? Depending on the goals and approach selected, what tone should he use in speaking with Amy in order to make it clear that the supervisor, not the employee, is conducting the meeting?

5. What directions should Jonathan give Amy? How should expectations for Amy's behavior be summarized?

Counseling is an opportunity to provide employees with direction in terms of their conduct and performance. Counseling is not just something that happens but is instead something that must be carefully planned to achieve maximum advantages for all participants. Remember that counseling should be done early and often. Waiting until bad habits have already become entrenched can make it much more difficult to correct behavior at a later date.

These are your choices:

1. You can choose to counsel an employee early and often, which will avoid having to correct problems concerning behavior or performance when they are much more difficult to solve.

2. You can choose to be well-prepared for an employee counseling session.

Chapter 7
Discipline

One of the most important roles of a supervisor is to maintain discipline in the workplace, which can also be one of the most difficult. Most supervisors did not sign on to be disciplinarians. In my experience, supervisors do not correct employee behavior too often, but rather too infrequently, as well as too late. As was discussed in the prior chapter on counseling, failure to timely discipline employees is, in the long run, not to the benefit of the employees.

Employees in the workplace watch to see how a supervisor handles disciplinary problems. Employees are very much in favor of the supervisor enacting fair and appropriate discipline for an employee who has broken the rules. An employee who is always late for work affects other employees. An employee who is rude and discourteous to other employees and their clients affects the success of the workplace. Your failure to address an employee's behavioral problems can have an adverse effect on employee productivity as well as their trust in you as a supervisor. Disciplining an employee is an important part of a supervisor's job, which involves choices about how well it is done.

Most likely your company or agency has an established discipline policy. However, one of the first decisions that you, as a supervisor, must make is what your personal philosophy of discipline may be. In most cases, disciplining an employee can only be initiated by the supervisor. What follows are some of the stereotypes that occur in the workplace with regard to how supervisors may or may not go about discipling employees:

1. The Don't Rock the Boat Supervisor

This type of supervisor has an easygoing approach to discipline. They do not want to be seen as a bad person by their employees, so they are lenient when it comes to behavioral problems. As long as everything is okay, they see no reason to rock the boat by disciplining an employee.

2. The Doesn't Want to Take the Time Supervisor

This type of supervisor does not want to invest the time it will take to discipline an employee. In many workplaces, supervisors will have to work with the Human Resources department in taking action. The human resources representative will ask a lot of questions, for which a supervisor will have to justify what they want to do. However, this all this takes time—time this supervisor is not interested in spending. The approach for this type of supervisor, is "Why bother."

3. The Throw the Book at Them Supervisor

This type of supervisor's first approach is just to fire the employee. They do not want to be bothered by a problem employee. In their mind, it is just easier to get rid of the employee. They, too, have no interest in spending the time necessary to work with the employee to try to improve their behavior.

4. The I Can't Take It Anymore Supervisor

This type of supervisor has let things go with the employee and ignored the behavior issues for too long, but now they just cannot take it anymore and move to take a final major action against the employee.

As the supervisor, it is your choice how you wish to maintain discipline in the workplace. You can choose to use one of the approaches above; or, instead, you can choose an approach that takes reasonable and fair actions when employees engage in behavior that is contrary to a workplace's rules.

As it happens, many workplaces do not have arbitration for employees to challenge a disciplinary action. However, the **Just Cause Standard** used by arbitrators provides a good analysis of whether an action taken against an employee is reasonable and fair. This standard is widely used in the federal, public, and private sectors where arbitration is available.

In determining whether the discipline of an employee is reasonable and fair, it is helpful to follow the **Seven Part Standard for Just Cause:**

Just Cause

1. The employee knew of the employer's policy.

- Employers enjoy a legal and contractual right to manage their workforce by establishing the rules and policies necessary to accomplish the mission. However, the employer has a fundamental obligation to inform

- the employees concerning the meaning and application of workplace rules.
- The employer must advise the employee that any act of misconduct or disobedience could result in discipline.
- The above statement should be made clear, be unambiguous, and inclusive of any possible penalties.

2. The employer's policy is reasonable.

- A workplace rule or policy must not be arbitrary, capricious, or discriminatory and must be related to the employer's stated goals and objectives.
- Even if the employee believes the policy or supervisory direction is unreasonable, the employee must obey, except in cases when doing so would jeopardize health or safety.

3. Was there a sufficient investigation?

- Did the employer conduct an investigation before making a decision about taking disciplinary and/or an adverse action?
- The employer is prosecutor, judge, and jury in discipline cases, and bears the full obligation to collect any and all facts that are relevant to the final decision.

4. Was the investigation fair and objective?

- The employer has the obligation to conduct a fair, timely, and thorough investigation that respects the employee's right to union representation, where available, and due process.

- Once completed, all facts must be evaluated with objectivity and be free from any bias or preconceived conclusion.

5. Substantial evidence exists that the employee violated the rule or policy.

- Did the investigation disclose any substantial proof or evidence that the employee was guilty of violating or disobeying a direct rule or order?
- Although there is no requirement of being preponderant, conclusive, or "beyond a reasonable doubt," any proof or evidence must be truly substantial.
- The investigation must be thorough and include a search for any evidence, even if it may clear the individual of wrongdoing.
- If an offense cannot be proven, then no action should ever be taken because any disciplinary action will then not be considered to be based on just cause.

6. The employer's policy has been consistently applied.

- Did the employer apply all rules, regulations, and penalties evenhandedly, and without discrimination to ALL employees?
- Were other employees who committed the same offense treated differently? If there was any evidence of discrimination or disparate treatment, both could automatically violate this test.

7. The discipline was reasonable and proportionate.

- Was the degree of discipline administered reasonably related to either the seriousness of the employee's offense or to the record of past service?
- A proven offense does not merit harsh discipline unless the employee has been proven guilty of the same (or other) offenses several times in the recent past.
- Although an employee's past record cannot be used to prove guilt in a current case, it can be used in determining the severity of discipline if guilt is established in the current case.
- Should two or more employees be found guilty of the same offense, their respective records can and should be used to determine their individual discipline. The employer has a right to give a lesser penalty to an employee whose employment record is not tainted with prior offenses, and this consideration should not be viewed as discriminatory. The reverse can also be true.
- The employee's offense may be excused through mitigating circumstances.

Levels of Discipline

In many circumstances, it is the choice of the supervisor whether to discipline an employee. In most workplaces, the supervisor has a choice as to what level of discipline to take when confronted with the misconduct of an employee. The disciplinary options available to a supervisor may, in the least severity, include counseling, either oral or in writing, or, in increased levels of severity, letters of reprimand, suspensions of a varying number of days, and finally, removal (firing) which is the most severe. In many workplaces, there is a belief in progressive discipline, which means starting with the least severe discipline appropriate for the misconduct, and then increasing the level of discipline if there is further employee misconduct. The idea is to start lower to give the employee the chance to improve their behavior. However, progressive discipline does not apply for offenses involving criminal behavior or serious misconduct, such as significant security breaches or extended AWOL.

Employee Counseling

The most frequently used approach to changing employee behavior is counseling. In most workplaces, counseling is the first step on the disciplinary ladder. When teaching supervisory training classes, I advise supervisors to counsel early and often when it comes to conduct and performance issues. Many supervisors dread counseling their employees. Counseling can have a negative connotation when considered as a precursor to disciplinary actions. However, counseling that is done well and taken seriously by the employee will actually negate the need for further action. If supervisors want to become effective counselors, then they must be prepared for the task. Counseling, however, should not occur in the form of an impromptu discussion. (See Chapter 5 for approaches to successful counseling.)

Firing Employees

On the other end of the spectrum from counseling is firing. Very few supervisors wake up in the morning and say to themselves, "I'm really looking forward to firing one of my employees today."

Firing, which some refer to as "industrial capital punishment," is not a step to be taken lightly. Firing has a major impact on the employee and their family. However, it can often be the right thing to do. If it is a government employee, then there are many due process systems that have to be navigated to be able to support the firing of a public or federal sector employee. These can be both complex and time-consuming. While many states have termination at will rules that make firing an employee considerably easier, employees have certain legal rights if the firing was done for illegal reasons, such as violations of Equal Employment laws.

There are good reasons why firing should not always be your first choice, as well as good reasons when it should be your first choice. For instance, there are significant costs involved in recruiting, hiring, and training employees. Additionally, the labor market may not have a good stock of employees with the job experience and skills needed for your workplace. If it is expensive to replace the employee and hard to find replacements, then options other than firing should be considered first. However, if the misconduct is so serious, then such financial considerations should not be used to justify not firing the employee. In making the decision about firing someone, at a minimum, the following should be considered:

1. Is the offense so serious that there is no viable alternative to firing?

2. Have efforts to change the employee's behavior been undertaken and failed?

3. Is there an illegal motivation for the action, such as firing based on race, sex, or religion?

In most workplaces, there are human resource staff to assist you in taking disciplinary actions that are consistent with the company policy. They are there to help with the disciplinary process, which is often new to many supervisors. While the human resources staff can assist with the process, the decision about whether to take discipline, as well as what level of discipline to impose, is the responsibility of the supervisor tasking the action. That supervisor must be able to justify the action taken and be comfortable living with the consequences.

These are your choices:

1. **You can choose to discipline employees when discipline is needed.**

2. **You can choose to take reasonable and fair disciplinary actions.**

3. **You can choose to be prepared when you counsel employees.**

4. **You can choose to fire employees when it is the right thing to do.**

Chapter 8
The Supervisor as Investigator

The investigation of workplace incidents is a common responsibility of supervisors. These are often called **administrative investigations** because they cover a broad range of investigations that do not involve criminal conduct. Workplace investigations may be conducted to determine whether an employer should take disciplinary action against an employee. An example is an investigation of an employee's tardiness to determine if discipline is warranted.

The Supervisor as Investigator

The most important component of a successful workplace investigation is the investigator. Being a good investigator requires skills, judgment, and integrity. You can be trained to have the skills and judgment required to successfully investigate workplace issues, but you cannot be trained to have integrity. Every supervisor questioning an employee about the employee's behavior or conduct is an investigator. The supervisor must know the limits of their authority to conduct an investigation. The supervisor must also know whether they are authorized to make a decision, or only to gather the facts that will be provided to the decisionmaker.

Gathering the Evidence

Almost all investigations involve gathering facts. Fact gathering involves both talking to people and obtaining documents. This fact gathering must be unbiased. A bias is a prejudice in favor or against a thing, person, or group. A supervisor must conduct an investigation in as neutral a manner as possible. Sometimes, investigators determine before the investigation what outcome they would like to have, and then conduct their investigation to prove their predetermined outcome. Such biased investigations undermine the integrity of the investigator. A management decisionmaker needs to know what the evidence is that supports taking action against an employee.

Characteristics of a Good Investigator

The number one characteristic of a good investigator is **preparation.** Good investigators thoroughly prepare prior to beginning an investigation. Preparation involves developing an investigative plan. An investigative plan is a written document that sets forth how the investigation is to be conducted and provides a checklist of things that must be accomplished. A plan further provides a means for organizing the investigation and making certain all-important issues are investigated.

One of the most important characteristics of a good investigator is their **honesty and integrity.** Honesty and integrity lead to an objective evaluation of the evidence, rapport with witnesses, and credibility in the eyes of the employees.

Another important characteristic of a good investigator is being **a good listener**. A good investigator listens to what a witness says and does not merely act as a note taker. Spending time listening, and not trying to take verbatim notes of what a witness says, allows an investigator to understand what is being said, while further not missing the body language of a witness while the witness is speaking.

Witnesses react to different investigators in different ways. They may tell one investigator considerably more than they tell another investigator. The difference is often based on how they are treated by the investigator and whether they trust the investigator. One major characteristic of a good investigator is the ability to **develop rapport** with the witnesses. Developing rapport is an important way to gain the trust of a witness. Rapport can be developed using certain words, tone inflection, gestures, facial expression, and stance as well as conversation.

A good investigator spends time thinking about what the evidence shows. A characteristic of a good investigator is to be able to **evaluate the evidence objectively,** so they see where the evidence is strong and where it is weak.

Investigators may hear things that they totally disagree with, or they may think the witness is "lying through their teeth" during an interview. However, while yelling at a witness or intimidating them may make for good TV drama, it is not a successful approach to obtaining testimony in a workplace investigation. Losing self-control when hearing suspected lies is the expression of a judgment on what is being said, one that effectively reduces any **credibility** the investigator might have had in the eyes of the witness.

Common Problems of Investigators

There are a number of common problems an investigator may encounter that could hinder their investigation. Some of these problems can be corrected with training; others may not be as easily remedied.

One of the biggest problems is that the investigation is **not thorough enough**. Failure to complete a thorough investigation is usually the result of lack of preparation. If the investigator does not know what they are looking for, the investigation may not be thorough enough. Another common reason for lack of thoroughness is that some investigators set a low bar on what they think is sufficient evidence. They then make great leaps from the evidence they have gathered to a barely sustainable conclusion.

Some investigators go to the opposite extreme. They do not feel comfortable making recommendations or conclusions without an exhaustive amount of evidence. They **investigate the issue to death**, not being sure they have enough evidence to support their recommendations or conclusions. Their investigations drag on as they try to tie down every possible issue or factual inconsistency.

Sometimes investigators go off on a tangent and **investigate the wrong issue**. They investigate issues which will not be helpful or necessary to resolve the actual issue being investigated. Sometimes, the wrong issue is investigated because the investigator has not done adequate research into what issues should be investigated.

The **ability to analyze facts** and then apply them appropriately to legal, regulatory, policy, or contractual standards is a necessary investigatory skill. An inability to properly analyze the facts is serious detriment to a proper investigation. If the investigator is investigating to determine whether there is just cause for a disciplinary action, the investigator must be able to analyze the facts, and then appropriately apply them to the just cause standard.

The conclusions and recommendations made by an investigator must be **based on the facts** gathered during the investigation. Making unsupported recommendations lessens the credibility of the investigator. If the facts do not support the recommendations and conclusions made by the investigator, any action based on them may not withstand the scrutiny of an arbitrator or judge.

You Can Be a Good Investigator

Conducting an investigation is hard work. If you are willing to put the work in, you will undoubtedly be a good investigator. It requires both skills as an investigator as well as solid judgment. One of the most important aspects of an investigation is preparation. Preparation requires developing an organized approach to conducting an investigation as well as an understanding of the issues to be investigated. You can be trained on how to prepare for an investigation. This preparation will usually take care of some of the common problems discussed above.

These are your choices:

1. **You can choose to be an unbiased investigator.**

2. **You can choose to be prepared to investigate a workplace issue.**

3. **You can choose to create rapport with witnesses to obtain information more effectively.**

4. **You can choose to be a good listener.**

Chapter 9
Managing Performance

An important role you have as a supervisor is to establish the expectations you have for your employees. Most employees will perform to the level expected of them—some well below, and some well above. To meet or exceed your expectations, employees must first know what these are. An employee cannot perform the amount and quality of work you expect unless they know your expectations. Therefore, you must decide whether you want to manage employee performance as they go along, or only provide an employee with a performance grade for how well they did after the work is completed.

Managing employee performance relies on the following essential supervisory activities:

- Planning work and setting expectations
- Continually monitoring performance
- Developing the employee's capacity to perform
- Periodically rating performance in a summary fashion
- Rewarding good performance

Planning work and setting expectations:

The supervisor decides the work and how it is to be done, how much work should be done, when the work should be completed, and the quality of the employee's work. In other words, these are the four basic job requirements a supervisor must make decisions on in order to ensure that their employees are performing effectively:

1. The work employees are expected to accomplish: what work do you expect employees to complete on a daily, weekly, monthly, or other basis?
2. The quantity of work employees should be completing: how much work should they be doing?
3. The quality of the work employees must produce: Is there a quality standard they must maintain?
4. When the work should be completed: What is the time period for finishing the work?

Let's take a closer look at the first requirement: what work the employee is supposed to do. At first, this may sound simple. You assign an employee work, and he or she completes it. Most employees know how to do their job. They understand and can perform the tasks assigned to them. However, sometimes, some employees just cannot do the work for various reasons. This situation can be one of the most difficult challenges for a supervisor.

You must make it clear to employees exactly what the work is that you expect them to do. One of the fundamental communication errors made by supervisors is not clearly communicating to employees what the expectations are for job performance. You may say, "of course, I tell them what they have to do." It is important to note, however, that telling employees what to do is not the same as explaining to each one precisely what you expect them to accomplish.

Quality Work

One of the hardest things to explain is quality work. Every job has a need for quality work by employees. Some jobs emphasize quality more than quantity or vice versa. Every job has some measure of quality involved. A bricklayer works mostly with their hands, but you can very easily tell the difference between one who does a good job and one who is not as skilled. A supervisor can tell the difference between quality decisions on claims and those which lack quality. Too many managers take the approach that when it comes to quality work, they know it when they see it. This approach, however, provides little to no help for an employee trying to meet a quality standard which may not exist other than in the mind of their supervisor. While this supervisor may know what quality looks like, for some reason they cannot explain it to an employee.

When I work with supervisors on devising performance management standards for a quality standard that employees are expected to achieve, I ask the supervisor to complete the following To Do List:

To Do List:

1. Look at one task that requires quality from your employees.
2. Write one sentence explaining what the quality standard is for this task.
3. Write the attributes of quality you would expect from an employee performing this task.

4. **After you have written the attributes, rewrite the initial sentence to conform to what is expected.**

5. **Test this sentence with an employee by asking the employee if they understand what they would have to do to produce quality work.**

Case Study:

It is helpful here to apply the above list to the following example of someone processing claims: The employee is told that his job is to process claims filed by insured customers. To do so, he is to use the company's claims manual to make decisions on the claims filed. He is expected to process twenty-five claims each day. He is to treat each claim fairly, while making a supportable decision. All this seems pretty straightforward. In this scenario, the employee knows 1) what he is supposed to do: process claims; 2) how many he is to do: twenty-five; 3) when he is to accomplish the work: daily; and 4) the expected quality standard: one that is consistent with the claims manual and supportable decisions.

On the surface, these instructions seem to cover all the bases. However, performance expectations are not always as easy as they seem. Here are some of the questions that also need to be answered. Does the employee have to do twenty-five per day, or can they average twenty-five per day? Are all claims the same amount of work? Are some claims harder than others? How do you know the decisions are consistent with the company's claims manual? How is quality review performed on the claims? A supervisor must be ready to answer all of these questions.

Continually Monitoring Performance

Setting expectations is important; however, monitoring an employee throughout the performance period is equally important. Meeting regularly to discuss an employee's performance should be part of an overall goal for providing an employee feedback on how they are performing. Ongoing monitoring provides the supervisor with the opportunity to check on how well employees are meeting predetermined standards, as well as to make changes to unrealistic or problematic standards.

One of the biggest mistakes a supervisor can make is not to spend time with their best performers. Too often, the greater part of supervisory time is given to improve the worst performers. While this time may marginally improve the weak performer, the same time spent with the high performer can actually end up as a more significant increase in office productivity.

Developing Capacity to Perform

Developing capacity means increasing the capacity to perform through training, providing assignments that introduce new skills or higher levels of responsibility, improving work processes, or other methods. Providing employees with training and developmental opportunities encourages good performance, strengthens job-related skills and competencies, and helps employees keep up with changes in the workplace, such as the introduction of new technology. Do your employees have all the tools they need to do the job? Your job is to provide those tools and assure that employees know how to use them. Most employees want to be successful in their jobs. They want to do a good job. Your job is to put them in the best position to be successful.

Rating Performance

After you tell employees what you want them to accomplish, you then have to evaluate if they were successful. An important part of helping an employee to be successful is having a good approach to evaluating employee performance. An employee assessment, performance appraisal, performance review, or performance evaluation is a method by which the performance of an employee is evaluated. It is a process of evaluation of employee performance and productivity in relation to certain pre-established criteria/standards to meet organizational objectives.

In some ways, the easiest thing to evaluate is to look at how much the employee did accomplish. In the example above, the employee had to complete twenty-five claims, so it is easy to keep track of how many claims the employee completed. The next requirement was that the claims be completed in a manner consistent with the claims manual. This is more difficult to assess. Instead of just counting the claims, you also have to make a quality judgment as to whether the claims decisions made by the employee are consistent with the company manual. This becomes a balance between quantity and quality. An employee may complete a lot of claims; however, they may be of poor quality, or the employee may provide excellent quality but completes fewer claims. You probably want both quality and quantity. Employees will do what they believe is expected of them. It is only a question of what you emphasize to them. If you want numbers, employees will try to give you good numbers. If you want quality decisions, employees will respond. If you want both, make certain your evaluation system clearly explains the balance between quality and quantity that you expect.

Rewarding Employees

In an effective organization, rewards are used often and well. Rewarding means recognizing employees for their performance, both individually and as members of groups, while acknowledging their contributions to the employer's mission. A basic principle of effective management is that all behavior is controlled by its consequences. Those consequences can and should be both informal and formal as well as both positive and negative.

Fairness in rewarding employees is something the employees will watch very carefully. If certain employees always get bonuses and others never get them, there will become a belief that certain employees are favorites, and others will never be rewarded. Employees who are never rewarded may give up and stop trying to do a better job. Having employees who always get bonuses, and then all of a sudden, they do not, can also lead to lower productivity. Rotating the bonuses each year, so each employee comes to expect a bonus when it is their turn does not lead to higher productivity, either, because the bonus is not tied to performance.

You have to decide how you want to reward employees. Are the awards truly based on performance, or are there some other criteria? Are awards fairly given? Do employees respect the award approach you take? Do employees understand the standards that must be met to receive an award? These are questions that should be asked.

These are your choices:

1. You can choose to be fair in evaluating employees, or just play favorites.

2. You can choose to monitor employees and provide them performance feedback throughout the evaluation period, or only provide them with an evaluation at the end of the period.

3. You can choose to set clearly understood performance expectations and seek employee input when establishing them.

4. You can choose to give employees rewards based on performance, or only give awards to your favorites.

Chapter 10
The Supervisor as Motivator

Does a supervisor actually motivate employees, or does a supervisor provide the environment where employees motivate themselves? Can you motivate someone, or do they motivate themselves? There is more to motivation, of course, than just these polarized examples. There are so many things written about motivation, one would have to be quite motivated to read them all. The question for each supervisor, then, is do you choose to do things that can motivate your employees, or do you take it for granted that they will motivate themselves? Different things motivate different employees. One employee may be motivated by money, and another may be motivated by recognition.

What follows are ten actions a supervisor can take to motivate employees or to provide them with an environment where they motivate themselves:

1. Provide employees with a clear picture of what is expected of them.

Knowing what is expected of them allows employees an understanding of what they should be striving to achieve. It is difficult for an employee to accomplish what you, as a supervisor, expect of them if it is not clear in their minds exactly what that may be. Most employees want to be successful. However, it is up to the supervisor to provide a clear path to success. Very few employees go to work wanting to do a lousy job. However, many go to work not having a clear picture of what they are to accomplish, and even more importantly, why. In today's world, we no longer have a workforce that is content with just taking orders. Instead, they want to know more about what is to be accomplished.

2. Provide the tools for employees to be successful.

Not having the necessary technology to accomplish their work efficiently can significantly reduce employees' effectiveness. It can also create frustration and lack of productivity. Beyond technology, the arrangement of the office and how it is equipped can lead to improved performance. The creation of an office environment that makes working easier can be conducive to employees being more successful.

3. Build trust.

Trust is most easily defined as a reliance on the honesty, dependability, and strength of character of someone. Trust is also faith in a person's abilities or words and includes the degree to which one believes that another person will look out for their best interests. When employees trust their supervisor, they are more productive. Some supervisors take it for granted that they are trusted but have never done the work to ensure trust. A breakdown in trust further leads to a breakdown in communication. A breakdown in communication additionally leads to a reduction in productivity.

One of the best ways to build trust is to show appreciation for the work of an employee. Appreciation makes an employee want to achieve more as well as to have more trust in their supervisor. One of the most common reasons employees leave their employment or transfer to another position is their relationship or lack of a relationship with their supervisor. And this often occurs because of a lack of trust.

4. Show Respect.

Respect is to think highly of someone as a result of their abilities, qualities, or achievements. There are various ways to show respect in the workplace. Complimenting an employee for a job well done is the surest way. Giving deference to their opinions is another. It can be quite clear to an employee when their supervisor does not respect them. By a supervisor's actions, it should also be equally clear when a supervisor respects an employee. Simply telling an employee that you respect their skills, attitude, or work ethic can be a powerful way of showing respect.

5. Show interest in the employees' careers.

Most employees are interested in advancing in their careers. It may be a promotion or a transfer to a job that they are interested in. Helping employees advance gives them the desire to do a better job. It shows they are more than just a widget hired to do a job. Employees blossom when mentored by their supervisor or other manager. A mentor is anyone who can share knowledge with a less-knowledgeable person and who can provide a mentee with insights, counsel, and life lessons beyond just the technical tasks. This type of mentor relationship helps employees when they have someone who is interested in them and their careers.

6. Offer training.

Training can be the building block to advancement and greater job satisfaction. Training that improves skills and makes an employee more eligible for promotion can incentivize them to do a better job.

7. Communicate often.

The more employees hear from their supervisor, the more likely they are to work effectively. Communication is the foundation of trust. The greater the communication, the greater the opportunity to build trust. Having effective meetings with employees can result in a greater understanding of the goals of the organization.

8. Give employees a chance to participate in solving workplace problems.

The more employees own the solutions to a workplace problem, the more they are likely to be intent on making their implementation successful. The less they participate in solving problems, the less they may be willing to ungrudgingly implement them. Most supervisors think of themselves as problem solvers. They know that if there is a problem, they will come up with a solution. However, there is always more than one way to solve a problem, and problems can be solved alone, with the input of other supervisors, or with employees. Much of the informal give and take in a workplace is actually collaborative problem-solving. Supervisors and employees often engage in informal as well as formal problem-solving processes that can either enhance communication or, when unsuccessful, lead to distrust. It is important to take advantage of opportunities to collaborate with your employees when collaboration makes sense for the workplace.

9. Explain the goals of the organization.

Employees need to know the big picture. How they fit in with the overall goals of the organization, and what those goals are must be communicated to them. Employees must understand why what they do is important. The more they understand the goals, the harder they will work to achieve them.

10. Reward employees.

Many employers think that money is what is the greatest motivator of employees. Employees must be appropriately compensated, or they will not be able to be retained by an employer. There are innumerable studies that show that of all the things that motivate employees, money is not on the top of the list for all employees. A sense of accomplishment often comes out on top. However, that is not to say that rewarding employees through compensation and bonuses does not provide motivation to some employees. Quite often, the recognition symbolized by a bonus or an award is what provides the motivation to many employees, and not the money itself.

It is easier to de-motivate than it is to motivate.

Many things a supervisor does may actually act to de-motivate employees. Avoiding de-motivators can be just as important as providing an environment that acts to motivate employees. For example, failing to recognize employees who believe they are deserving of recognition is a good way to de-motivate the employees. If the employees are not deserving, the reasons should be explained to them. Paying someone less than another employee doing the same work can also de-motivate employees. However, policies such as fairness and transparency in monetary awards and salary setting can counteract beliefs that can de-motivate employees.

These are your choices:

1. You can choose to motivate or de-motivate employees.

2. You can choose to work to build trust or take it for granted that employees trust you and be surprised when they do not.

3. You can choose to make employees a part of solving workplace problems, or simply dictate all aspects of their work.

4. You can choose to communicate with your employees.

5. You can choose to be fair and transparent in rewarding employees.

Chapter 11
What Do You Know about Employment Law and Discrimination?

There are different laws that apply in the various states concerning employment issues. Some states are **termination at will** states that allow an employer to terminate the employment relationship at any time for any, or no, reason at all. Termination at will does not apply to employees of the federal government, but it does apply in many states. There are, however, exceptions to this broad employment right that vary from state-to-state.

At-will employment is a term used in private sector labor law for contractual relationships in which an employee can be dismissed by an employer for any reason (that is, without having to establish just cause for termination), and without warning, as long as the reason is not illegal (e.g., firing because of the employee's race, religion, or sexuality). When an employee is acknowledged as being hired at-will, courts deny the employee any claim for loss resulting from the dismissal. The rule is justified by its proponents on the basis that an employee may be similarly entitled to leave their job without reason or warning. The practice is viewed as unjust by those who see the employment relationship as characterized by an inequality of bargaining power.

Employees in every state and the federal government are entitled to the protections against employment discrimination, which can be found in the Title VII of the Civil Rights Act. They cannot be fired or have other workplace actions taken against them if the employer has engaged in discriminatory practices in violation of Title VII. These discriminatory practices may have been as result of the actions of a supervisor.

Title VII applies to employers with fifteen or more employees, including state and local governments. It also applies to employment agencies and labor organizations, as well as to the federal government. The law forbids discrimination when it comes to any aspect of employment, including hiring, firing, salary, job discrimination in terms of reassignments, promotions, layoffs, training, fringe benefits, and any other terms or condition of employment.

Supervisors, however, cannot be held personally liable in damages for engaging in employment discrimination. If there are monetary damages, they are the responsibility of the employer. However, a supervisor who engages in employment discrimination may be subject to removal or other discipline by their employer.

A type of discrimination that has been become prevalent in recent years is sexual harassment. With the advent of the Me-Too movement, sexual harassment has moved to center stage in many discrimination-based workplace disputes. However, sexual harassment as a violation of law existed long before the Me-Too movement. The law has not changed as a result of this new movement, although an increased awareness of the right for employees to complain about sexual harassment has. Sexual harassment has always been wrong, but what has changed is that, today, employees may not be as reluctant to raise a claim as they may have been in the past.

Unfortunately, many supervisors still do not fully understand what sexual harassment is and how it affects employees in the workplace. For example, many managers do not know that sexual harassment occurs not only between men and women, but it can also occur between persons of the same sex.

First, it is important to note that sexual harassment has several deleterious effects on workers who are either victimized by or exposed to it. Those who are subjected to sexual harassment often experience emotional and physical symptoms for years following the events. The effect of these symptoms can have a major impact not only on the lives of those directly affected, but also on workplace productivity. Sexual harassment affects all workers, and its true costs include:

- Decreased Productivity
- Increased Turnover
- Reputational Harm
- Decreased Morale

According to the U.S. Equal Employment Opportunity Commission (EEOC), sexual harassment can occur in a variety of ways:

- The victim, as well as the harasser, can either be a man or a woman—a victim does not have to be of another gender.
- The harasser may be the victim's supervisor, an agent of the employer, a supervisor in another area, a co-worker, or a non-employee, such as a vendor or customer.
- The victim does not have to be only the person being harassed but could also be anyone affected by the offensive conduct.
- Unlawful sexual harassment may occur without economic injury to, or discharge of, the victim.
- The harasser's conduct must be unwelcome.

Sexual harassment can include unwelcome sexual advances, requests for sexual favors, and other verbal or physical harassment of a sexual nature. This includes physical, verbal, or non-verbal conduct of a sexual nature, such as:

- Unwanted sexual attention
- Sexual advances
- Requests for sexual favors
- Sexually explicit comments
- Other conduct of a sexual nature

Examples of conduct that could be considered sexual harassment:

- **Denying an Employment Benefit**—Denying (directly or indirectly) an employment benefit or employment-related opportunity to an employee for refusing to comply with a sexually-oriented request.
- **Threatening Denial of an Employment Benefit**—Threatening (directly or indirectly) to deny an employment benefit or an employment-related opportunity to an employee for refusing to comply with a sexually-oriented request.
- **Providing or Promising an Employment Benefit (Quid Pro Quo)**—Providing or promising (directly or indirectly) to provide an employment benefit or employment-related opportunity to an employee in exchange for complying with a sexually-oriented request.
- **Engaging in Physical Contact**—Engaging in sexually explicit or suggestive physical contact, including touching another employee in a way that is unwelcome or restricts an employee's movement.

- **Displaying or Transmitting Pornography**—Displaying or transmitting pornographic or sexually oriented materials, such as photographs, posters, cartoons, drawings, or other images, or storing or accessing such materials on government-owned equipment or employer-owned equipment for personal use or consumption.
- **Engaging in Indecent Exposure or Exposing Body Parts to Attract Sexual Attention**—Engaging in indecent exposure of body parts usually kept private in order to attract sexual attention. Exposing body parts to attract sexual attention could include a low-cut blouse or tight pants.
- **Making Obscene Gestures**—Making obscene gestures of a sexually-oriented nature.
- **Making Romantic Advances**—Making romantic advances toward an individual and persisting, despite rejection of the advances.
- **Using Sexually Oriented Language**—Using sexually-oriented language or making sexually-related propositions, jokes, or remarks, including graphic verbal commentary about an individual's body or clothing.
- **Sending Sexual Messages**—Sending sexually suggestive or obscene messages by mail, in person, by telephone, text, or any other electronic communication.

Importantly, understanding sexual harassment is not just about staying out of trouble, but also truly valuing all employees in the workplace, regardless of gender. A good manager therefore needs to know how certain actions may be perceived in order to ensure that all employees have a workplace where they are valued for what they contribute, and where they are not demeaned or treated inappropriately because of their gender.

Anti-discrimination laws further prohibit harassment against individuals in retaliation for filing a discrimination charge, testifying, or participating in any way in an investigation, proceeding, or lawsuit, or opposing employment practices that they reasonably believe discriminate against individuals.

The EEO laws prohibit punishing job applicants or employees for asserting their rights to be free from employment discrimination, including sexual harassment. Asserting these EEO rights is called "protected activity," and it can take many forms. For example, it is unlawful to retaliate against applicants or employees for

- Filing or being a witness in an EEO charge, complaint, investigation, or lawsuit;
- Communicating with a supervisor or manager about employment discrimination, including harassment;
- Answering questions during an employer investigation of alleged harassment;
- Refusing to follow orders that would result in discrimination; or
- Resisting sexual advances or intervening to protect others.

Engaging in EEO activity, however, does not shield an employee from all discipline or discharge. Employers are free to discipline or terminate workers if the employer is motivated by non-retaliatory and/or non-discriminatory reasons. However, an employer is not allowed to do anything in response to EEO activity that would discourage someone from resisting or complaining about future discrimination.

When a claim of sexual harassment is received by a manager or supervisor, the way in which it is handled matters greatly for both the employer and the employee. If a claim is improperly handled, it can have a major impact on the employee's trust in the management of the organization, and can even create greater liability for the employer.

When receiving a complaint of sexual harassment, the manager/supervisor should be mindful of the following:

- Employees do not have to use exact words, such as "harassment," when making a claim that warrants employer action, so managers must understand the concern well enough to determine whether the issue should be treated as an allegation of harassment or hostile work environment.

- The first thing to do is NOT ignore it. Once someone comes forward to a manager, the employer is now considered to be put on notice. Being on notice creates legal liability for the employer's actions, particularly if nothing is done about a legitimate claim. The manager receiving the claim, therefore, should listen and take the concern seriously, while also being professional and nonjudgmental. However, the manager is not supposed to determine the validity of the complaint, but rather only gather enough facts to be able to forward the matter for investigation.

    Whenever an employee speaks with a manager about a claim of sexual harassment, the manager should contact the Human Resources office to be advised of the employer's protocol.

- Resist making statements that imply a judgment or position, such as: "maybe he or she didn't mean it," "maybe you should not dress that way," or "maybe you should not have responded the way you did."

- Assure that the alleged victim is aware of available employer resources, such as counseling services.

- Assure that the alleged victim is aware that anonymity cannot be guaranteed.

- Ask the alleged victim if they would like to be temporarily moved to a different location (or telework) during pendency of the investigation.

- Assure that the alleged victim is aware of their right to seek redress through formal processes, such as a union grievance or EEO complaint.

Here are some good and bad ideas for how to handle sexual harassment and retaliation complaints and investigations:

Bad idea: Changing the alleged victim's hours, duties, and physical location, etc., without communicating with them and working through interim measures, which can be viewed as retaliation.

Bad idea: Focusing on what the alleged victim wants or the hype surrounding an accusation versus what the facts show.

Bad idea: Doing something that management assumes will be beneficial to the alleged victim without asking or communicating with the person (this can lead to retaliation complaints).

Good idea: Advising witnesses, including the alleged victim, that, due to privacy concerns, they will not be advised by the investigator of the outcome of the investigation and whether or not corrective action was taken (in other words, manage expectations).

Good idea: During or after the investigation, and separate from the specific complaint under investigation, assess the environment to determine the root causes and whether an office-wide refresher sexual harassment training may be warranted.

Good idea: Do not become the morality police; instead, assess what the impact is to the workplace.

Good idea: During or after the investigation, assess whether spin-off corrective action is warranted; for example, a manager was aware of the inappropriate conduct and did nothing to intervene or manage it since no one had complained.

These are your choices:

1. You can choose not to sexually harass your employees.

2. You can choose not to engage in any discrimination in violation of Title VII of the Civil Rights Act of 1964.

3. You can choose to value all your employees without regard to race, color, religion, sex and national origin, with any aspect of employment, including hiring, firing, salary, job discrimination in terms of reassignments, promotions, layoffs, training, fringe benefits, and any other terms or condition of employment.

Chapter 12
Things Supervisors Should Not Do

When first becoming a supervisor, it can be difficult to know exactly what the right things to do may be and what the wrong things may be. In addition to making the right choices, making the wrong choices, too, can have a significant impact on your effectiveness as a supervisor. With so much to learn as a supervisor, it can sometimes happen that things you should absolutely avoid get overlooked.

What follows is a list of some actions and behaviors that a supervisor should avoid:

1. **Do not comment on confidential information.**

    There are three kinds of confidential information that you should protect: 1) employee information, 2) management information, and 3) business information. Do not be someone who leaks information. Knowing inside information can be a powerful thing; however, leaking that information can be a disaster both for you as an individual and for your company. For instance, if you have been entrusted with information about an employee's health, sharing that information with other employees can have a significantly negative impact on that employee as well as what other employees think of you.

2. **Do not make exceptions for employer rules and policies for your close friends or family members.**

    Do not be blind to the rules and policies of your employer

just because of a friendship with an employee or a family member at work. Doing so is unethical. Playing favorites is one of the most disliked traits a supervisor can have, and it further undermines the supervisor's credibility in the workplace.

3. **Do not let your ego take control.**

    When you get caught in your ego, it will gradually reduce the effectiveness of your role as a supervisor as well the effectiveness of your company. The success of an enterprise does not lie on any one person's shoulders. Therefore, know what the needs of each team member are to be able to help everyone reach their main goal. If, instead, you broadcast or insinuate that you are the reason everything is going so well, you will easily loose the support of those who work for you.

4. **Do not think and act as if you know everything.**

    Similar to letting your ego take control, a know-it-all also cannot be an effective supervisor. While it is a great advantage for a supervisor to be considered smart, it is a disadvantage to make employees feel that they are not smart and offer little towards the success of the organization.

5. **Do not make comments about an employee to someone else.**

    Avoid gossip. Supervisors should not talk about the behavior or performance of an employee with anyone else. If you talk about other employees, and especially if what you say about them is derogatory, the employees who hear your comments will often think you are also talking about them.

6. **Do not allow personal relationships to influence you.**

    When it comes to evaluating an employee, supervisors should be both objective and fair. Employees want to believe that their supervisor is judging them on the merits, and not based on relationships that have nothing to do with the work they are doing. The more you play favorites, the lower you will be viewed in the eyes of the employees you supervise.

7. **Do not approve unsatisfactory performance for an employee who has been through a hard time.**

    While it is okay to empathize with an employee when they have admitted they are experiencing personal problems, this should not be an excuse to approve unsatisfactory performance. Instead, you should acknowledge the unsatisfactory performance, while working with the employee on a plan to fix the deficiencies.

8. **Do not diagnose or give advice to an employee concerning their personal problems.**

    Even if you studied psychology, if you were not hired to be a psychologist, then you should not give any advice on personal problems or behavior to your employees. The person who helps an employee with their personal problems is a friend, not a supervisor. Supervisors are not friends with their employees.

9. **Do not moralize or make value judgments of others.**

   Overall, it is better to respect the privacy and personal life of employees. You may not personally like an employee because of the life choices the employee has made; however, if their choices have not had a detrimental effect on the workplace, and those choices are not otherwise illegal or contrary to company policy, these should not be considered when evaluating the employee. This is especially true when working in a diverse environment with many different kinds of people.

10. **Do not allow behavior that could be dangerous to another person.**

    Do not let any action jeopardize your employees at work. For example, it is illegal for anyone in the workplace to harass any person at work—physically, sexually or mentally. Therefore, supervisors should always keep their team compliant with the law.

11. **Do not allow genuine concern for an employee to interfere with the management of their performance.**

    You are not an employee's brother, sister, mother, father, priest, minister, rabbi, or psychologist. If an employee is having personal problems, it is not your job to try to fix those problems. Instead, your job is to be fair in the treatment of the employee. If available, send the employee-to-employee assistance programs that may better deal with the employee's issues. You job as supervisor is to show empathy, while not allowing the employee's problems interfere with your effectively supervising the overall workforce.

These are your choices:

1. **You can choose not to do any of the things on the above list.**

Chapter 13
A Good Supervisor Has a Philosophy

A personal philosophy is a framework that helps you both to understand who you are and to make sense of your life. A philosophical framework helps to guide you in how you act and the decisions that you make. While we often do not realize it, we all have a personal philosophy. Similarly, you will also need to develop a philosophy as a supervisor because you will need to have a framework that guides your supervisory approach and actions.

Many supervisors may have already adopted a framework for dealing with employees based on their own personal experiences of being managed by their past supervisors, with varying results. This chapter provides you with the opportunity to make a choice about what philosophy you would like to use as your framework.

Two Basic Philosophies

Deciding on your philosophy of supervising is an important choice. There are two basic philosophies: 1) **compliance** and 2) **collaboration**. There is also a third philosophy, which is a combination of the first two, or both compliance and collaboration.

Compliance is based on the concept of ordering an employee to do something, and then holding them accountable for what was ordered to be done. A philosophy of compliance is based on the idea that a supervisor should direct employees as to what they are to do and hold them accountable for their performance by evaluating how well they comply with the directions. This approach leaves major decisions in the supervisor's hands, while allowing for only minimal input from employees. If employees do not comply with the supervisor's directions, they will face negative consequences. Compliance is often used when supervisors try to force change on employees.

Collaboration is an approach to supervision that entails the supervisor and employee problem- solving together to come up with the best approach to work through issues. A philosophy of collaboration involves engaging employees when decisions are to be made. Collaboration is usually used when supervisors wish to foster change through employee support, which, in turn, can create a good work environment for employees. This approach requires significant input from employees, who must take active responsibility for assisting in the problem-solving process. A supervisor, of course, cannot engage in collaborative problem solving alone. It takes the active engagement of employees. Additionally, successful collaborative problem-solving may require training for both supervisors and employees.

Your responsibility as a supervisor is to know when to use compliance, and when to use collaboration. You must have the flexibility to use either approach as necessary based on the needs of the work being done. It is your choice whether to problem solve a solution to a work problem, or to simply tell employees how you want an issue handled. Making the correct choice depends on the nature of the problem. Making the right choice for a specific problem can greatly improve your effectiveness as a supervisor.

Compliance

All supervisors know that getting the job done is the highest priority. How you get it done can have a big impact on your success as a supervisor. Knowing how to use a compliance approach successfully is an important skill. Providing directions for new assignments and tasks is a normal part of the role of a supervisor or manager. What follows are effective ways to direct employees:

1. Be specific when assigning tasks. Employees need to understand both when a task is to be completed and how it is expected to be done. Therefore, be certain to create an atmosphere where an employee is not afraid of asking questions when they do not understand what they are to accomplish. Provide your employees with a chance to ask questions. Offer them the opportunity to clarify their questions. This step helps to strengthen communication between the employee and supervisor, and thus improves the probability of a successful outcome. The employee then has the opportunity to confirm that they fully understand what is being asked of them.

Here is an example of what happens when tasks are not clearly understood by employees who fear questioning the supervisor:

Early one afternoon, Eric receives an email from Nina, his direct supervisor, asking him to complete a particular task "ASAP." Based on his previous experiences with Nina, Eric does not question the meaning of "as soon as possible" and assumes that this must be an emergency. Although he is currently working on a weekly report to be submitted to headquarters later that day, he puts it aside in order to prioritize Nina's task. As a result, when the weekly report is turned in late, headquarters reprimands Nina and the entire branch office.

Nina is angry that Eric did not complete the weekly report on time. She believes that he should have understood that the email task was not nearly as important. When Nina tells Eric how unhappy she is, he explains that he thought that she had needed the "ASAP task" immediately. Nina calls HR to take a disciplinary action against Eric for not completing the weekly report on time. When HR asks Nina what "ASAP" meant, she replies, "Eric should have known that it did not mean handing in the weekly report late." Although Eric has always understood the importance of submitting work to headquarters on time, he believes that he followed instructions by giving the "ASAP task" priority over the weekly report. Long ago, when he had asked Nina which tasks should be done first, Nina had told Eric that someone at his pay level should be "able to figure out" how to prioritize his tasks. He should not need to talk to her each time a task is assigned.

In this situation, both parties made assumptions, but neither attempted to confirm whether or not those assumptions were correct. Because making assumptions is often easier than addressing issues, some people will rely upon their own assumptions about other people's wants, needs, and motivations. Unfortunately, these assumptions are frequently incorrect and can actually create disputes in the workplace. Things that start out as misunderstandings can therefore escalate into a serious problem between supervisors and employees. The best way to avoid assumptions is to create a workplace climate where employees never fear asking questions. In our scenario Eric was afraid of asking questions because it would make him look like he did not know how to do his job therefore he assumed the ASAP project was his top priority.

2. How you give directions can have an effect on the success of an employee. Actions, such as your tone of voice, word choice, and body language, can help gain support for what needs to be accomplished.

Here is an example of how to give employees directions:

Contrast these statements: "Get this done, now!" and "Sam, it is crucial to the success of the project for you to get this done quickly. I know you are busy with other things, but this has to be a priority to help accomplish the mission. Thanks for understanding that it has to be done right now." What can be perceived in the initial statement as yelling at an employee is not as successful as the following statements explaining the need for prompt action. There is little doubt the latter approach would be perceived as positive and the former as negative. When you take the time to explain the business importance of the task you are requesting to be completed, you are both teaching and showing respect for the employee you asked to complete the work.

3. Trust your employees. Resist the urge to oversee or micromanage an employee's completion of the requested task.

Many organizations spend a fair share of their budgets on upgrading computer hardware and software in an effort to increase productivity. IT improvements are easy to implement. You order the equipment, install it, and then train employees on how to use it. Any productivity gains can be easily monitored, too. However, implementing, assessing, and valuing increased trust in the workplace are more complicated. Most managers understand the inherent value of supervisor-employee trust; however, translating that into saved costs or gains in output might seem impossible.

As a solution to that problem, Stephen M. R. Covey's, **The Speed of Trust**, explains how to quantify the value of trust for increased productivity in the workplace. Covey posits that there are quantifiable dividends in the form of increased employee productivity in workplaces where supervisors and employees trust one another. On the other end of the spectrum, when trust is absent in a workplace, organizations are taxed in the form of diminished output. Leading effectively is learning to trust that your team can complete tasks without you.

Collaboration

If you are a supervisor, think of a workplace problem that you are currently having and how problem-solving with your employees would develop a sound solution as well as a more successful workplace. If you are an employee, think of how you can assist in solving a workplace problem through collaboration with your supervisor. What follows are five basic steps for collaborative supervisor-employee problem-solving:

1. Identify issues

Each participant in the problem-solving process must have a clear understanding of what issue needs resolving. Defining the issue at the beginning will greatly improve chances for success.

For example, Tucker, who supervises the Accounting reports section, is concerned that his employee's reports are being turned in late. He has two options. On the one hand, he can warn employees that if reports continue to be late, consequences will result. In order to successfully use this compliance approach, Tucker must know exactly what he wants done, and his employees must obey completely. On the other hand, Tucker can try to find out why the reports are consistently late. If he chooses this collaborative option to work with his employees, then he should meet with them to discuss the problem.

2. Identify interests

Before the meeting, Tucker should notify employees of its purpose, so that they can prepare to work together. Each participant should identify their own needs to be satisfied, as well as what concerns must be addressed in order to reach a successful solution. Importantly, this process is based on explanation, not justification.

To open the discussion, Tucker should look for reasons, and not solutions, by asking his employees why the reports are not being submitted on time. As the supervisor, Tucker's main interest is the work being accomplished on time. The employees' interest is not only accomplishing the work, but also having adequate time to devote to the task. By soliciting his employees' opinions, Tucker will discover their reasons for the late reports.

3. Develop options

Group brainstorming will allow Tucker and his employees to formulate options for getting the reports done on time. Tucker should ask for possible solutions from each participant, and all options should be discussed. For example, one option might be to change the submission deadlines for the reports. Another option might be to lessen the amount of information to be covered. A third option might be to require that all employees check in with Tucker on a regular basis.

4. Develop standards

Standards are a strainer through which we run all options to weigh their value as solutions. Standards will help determine which options make the most sense. Examples of a standard could be cost-effectiveness, efficiency, or fairness.

5. Judge options according to the standards

Each option should be judged according to the standards. In Tucker's situation, if one option involves hiring additional staff when the standard is cost-effectiveness, then this option is clearly not the most appropriate. While all participants in the problem-solving process should be involved in judging options, the supervisor will make the final decision.

This problem-solving process will further create the byproducts of increased communication and trust, which will lead to a more collaborative work environment. By engaging employees in solving problems, supervisors create opportunities for transparency, which is essential for developing, increasing, and maintaining trust. However, collaborative problem-solving is not intended to replace a supervisor or employee's accountability for the implemented solutions.

Employee Engagement

As a supervisor, whichever philosophy you choose, compliance or collaborative, you should still consider encouraging employee engagement in the workplace. High levels of employee engagement in an organization are linked to superior business performance, including increased profitability, productivity, employee retention, customer metrics, and safety levels. An engaged employee is defined as one who is fully absorbed by and enthusiastic about their work, and so they take positive action to further the organization's reputation and interests. Communication and trust are important to the development of engaged employees.

Here are some tips on how to encourage engaged employees:

1. Communicate clear goals and expectations.
2. Share information and numbers.
3. Encourage open communication.

4. Recognize that not communicating or communicating late can damage engagement.
5. Develop trust in the employees for the organization and its managers.
6. Provide constant feedback on the positives.
7. Give immediate feedback.
8. Show how feedback is being used.
9. Collaborate on and share problem-solving with employees.
10. Celebrate achievements.

If, as a supervisor, you want to have engaged employees, then you must also have both good communication and trust in your workplace. While engagement is the newest approach to having a more successful workforce, it really just comes down to the basics of the effectiveness of your communication. In addition, the employees must trust the organization, and, most importantly, its managers and supervisors.

These are your choices:

1. You can choose a compliance philosophy of supervising.
2. You can choose a collaborative philosophy of supervising.
3. You can choose to be able to use either a compliance or problem-solving approach, depending on which one meets the needs of the task you are trying to accomplish.
4. You can choose to have engaged employees.

Chapter 14
What Do I Do Now?

There are all kinds of choices that need to be made to be an effective supervisor. While reading this book, at times you may have felt a bit overwhelmed by all the choices. However, the most important choice to make is whether you want to be a good supervisor, a bad supervisor, or merely a mediocre supervisor. You cannot rely on your employer to make these choices for you; you must decide these for yourself. As this book has outlined, there are many choices you can make; however, it is important to note that the choices outlined in this book need not be applied all at once. Instead, the initial challenge is just to get started making the necessary choices that will help you to become the supervisor you want to be.

About the Author

Joseph Swerdzewski obtained his undergraduate degree in 1971 from the College of the Holy Cross, Worcester, Massachusetts. He received his law degree from Fordham University Law School in 1974. He is licensed to practice law in New York and Colorado. He began his legal career as a Judge Advocate in the United States Air Force at Vandenberg AFB, California. While leaving active duty he remained in the Air Force Reserve retiring as a Lieutenant Colonel. In 1979 he joined the Federal Labor Relations Authority (FLRA) as a supervisory attorney for the Los Angeles Region. He became the Regional Attorney of the Denver Region of the FLRA in 1982. As Regional Attorney he was responsible for the investigation and prosecution of unfair labor practice charges in a 12-state region. He was named Counsel for Special Outreach of the FLRA in 1990. In this role he developed innovative dispute resolution and training programs for the Office of General Counsel.

In 1993 he was appointed General Counsel of the FLRA by President William J. Clinton after confirmation by the United States Senate. He was appointed by President Clinton and confirmed by the Senate for a second term in 1998. He is the only General Counsel to be appointed for a second term. As General Counsel he was responsible for the investigation and prosecution of unfair labor practice violations worldwide. He is well known for his advice and policy memorandums on labor relations topics for the federal sector, which he issued, while General Counsel. His creative approaches to developing alternative dispute resolution processes resulted in a thirty percent (30%) decrease in unfair labor practice filings during his tenure. He is a much sought-after speaker, having given over 300 speeches and seminars on labor relations topics throughout the United States and South Korea, Italy and Panama.

In 2001 he left the FLRA to become President and CEO of FPMI Solutions, a federal government contractor specializing in human resource outsourcing and training. He led FPMI through a significant expansion of its federal business, including winning a contract to hire all the staff for the Transportation Security Administration (TSA) nationwide. In 2004 he successfully guided the company through a sale to a Washington based equity investment firm. In 2005 he left FPMI and started JSA - Joseph Swerdzewski and Associates, LLC., a human resource consulting and training firm (www.jsafed.com). He spent time as a member of the Adjunct Faculty of the University of Alabama – Huntsville lecturing in the School of Business Administration. He served as Team Leader for Obama-Biden Transition Team. In this role he was responsible for the Agency Review of the Federal Labor Relations Authority.

Other Books by Joseph Swerdzewski

THE ESSENTIAL GUIDE TO FEDERAL LABOR RELATIONS ~ What you need to know to be successful

The Essential Guide to Federal Labor Relations gives your Managers, Supervisors, Labor Relations Practitioners, and Union Representatives an in-depth understanding of labor relations concepts. This easy-to-read comprehensive guide is essential for practitioners and those actively involved in day-to-day labor relations.

A Guide to Successful Federal Sector Collective Bargaining

Everything Managers, Supervisors, and Union Representatives need to know about Collective Bargaining in the Federal Sector!
Here is a partial list of topics covered: Federal Sector Bargaining Processes, Duty to Bargain, Scope of Bargaining, Procedures and Appropriate Arrangements, The Change Bargaining Process, Ground Rules for Bargaining, Preparation for Bargaining, Language in a Collective Bargaining Agreement, Official Time, Alternative Work Schedules, How to Negotiate, and Relationship of the Parties.

COMMUNICATION AND TRUST ~ A GUIDE TO A SUCCESSFUL WORK PLACE

This book is sure to help Managers, Employees, and Union Representatives everywhere build better relationships in the work place.
Learn to develop more effective communication skills!
Learn how communication and trust work hand-in-hand in the workplace.
Read real life workplace scenarios where communication went wrong and learn what to do in similar situations.

HOW TO CONDUCT A WORKPLACE INVESTIGATION

Everything your Managers, Supervisors, Union Representatives, and Lawyers need to know about workplace investigations! Here is a partial list of topics covered: The Investigator's Authority, Common Problems of Investigators, Developing an Investigative Plan, Investigator Communication Skills, Evidence, Conduct and Role of an Investigator, Preparation for an Investigation, Interviewing and/or Questioning Witnesses, Witness Right and Representation, and Investigative Reports.

Understanding Sexual Harassment – What Managers Need to Know About Sexual Harassment

A Guide to Sexual Harassment and Retaliation Claims and Investigations for Supervisors, Managers, Employees, and Union Representatives

This book explains what can be considered workplace sexual harassment. Many managers do not fully understand what sexual harassment is and how it effects employees in the workplace. Many employees have heard of sexual harassment but are not aware of what it means to them. Beyond providing an understanding of what sexual harassment is, how to investigate and generally respond to claims of sexual harassment will be explained.

www.ingramcontent.com/pod-product-compliance
Lightning Source LLC
Chambersburg PA
CBHW060343170426
43202CB00014B/2862